Help the dogs find their bones by cutting each line.

Lead the chicks back to their mother by cutting each line.

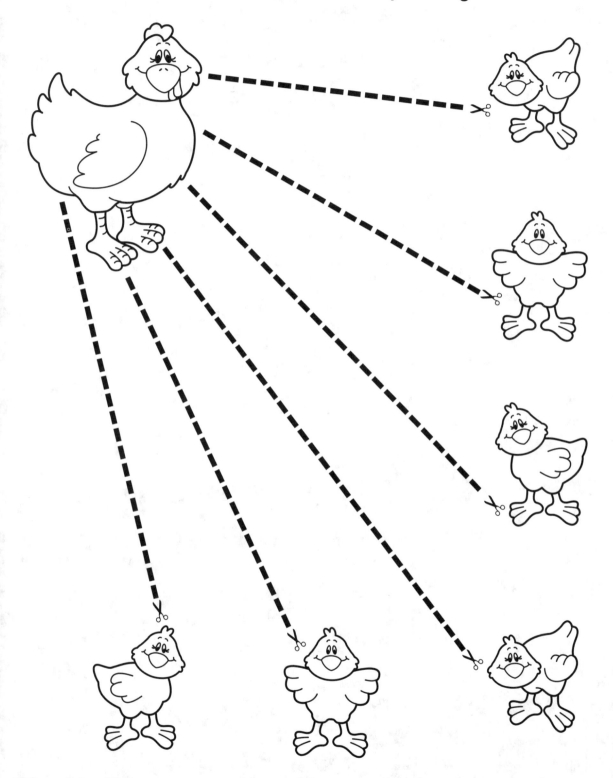

3

Help the birds find their nests by cutting each line.

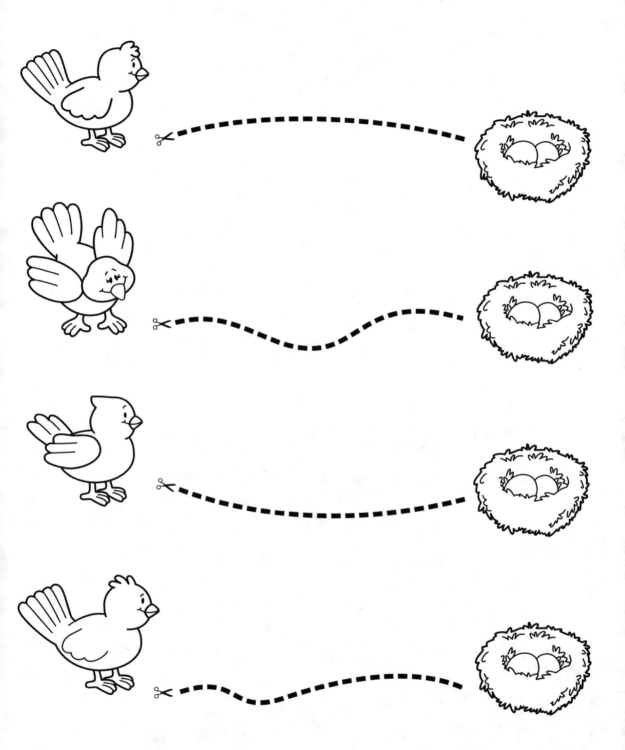

Help the bees find their honey pots by cutting each line.

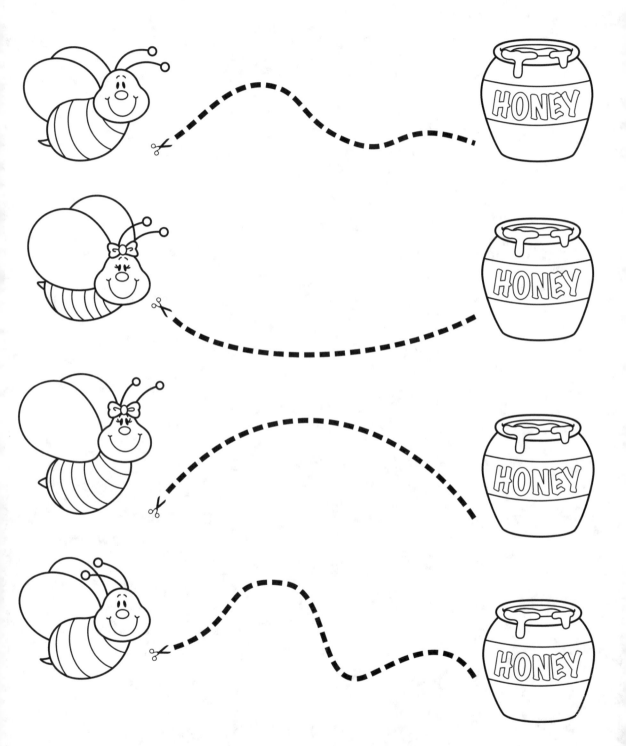

Lead the mice to the cheese by cutting each line.

Help the children catch the baseballs by cutting each line.

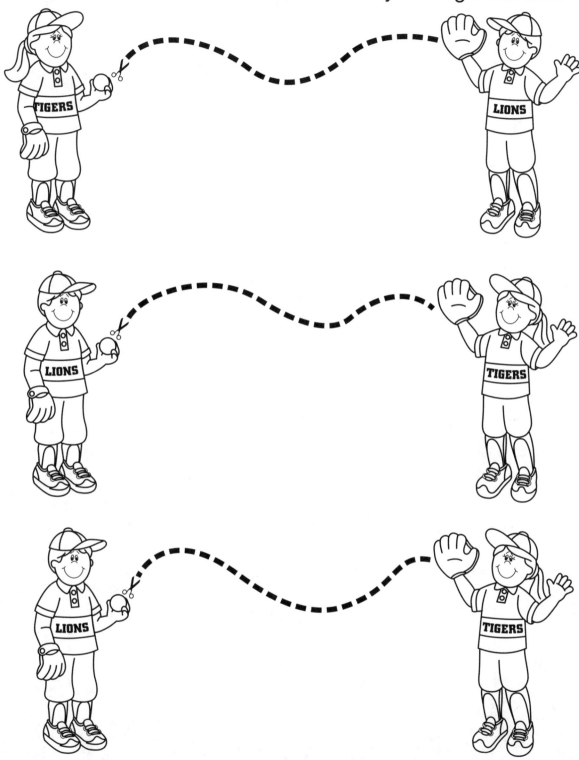

Lead the cats to their balls of yarn by cutting each line.

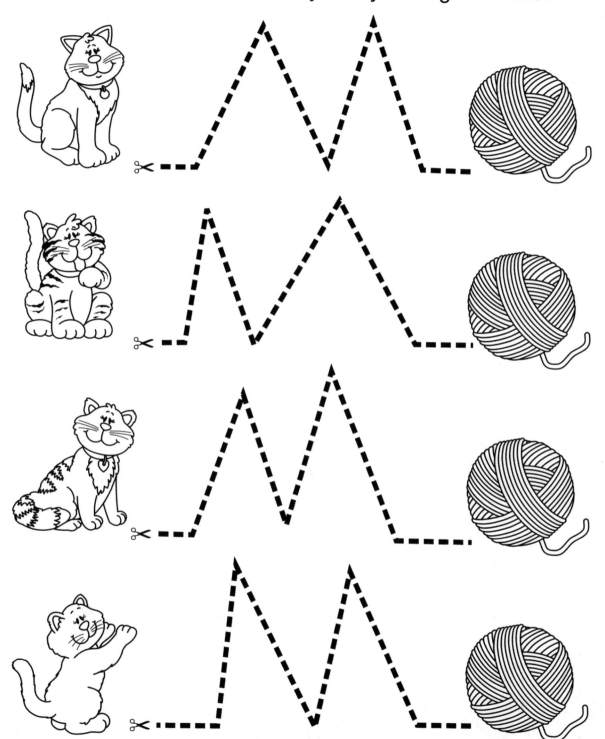

13

Help Andy the astronaut find his rocket by cutting the line.

Color the airplane. Then, cut on the dashed line and fold on the thick line. The airplane will stand up.

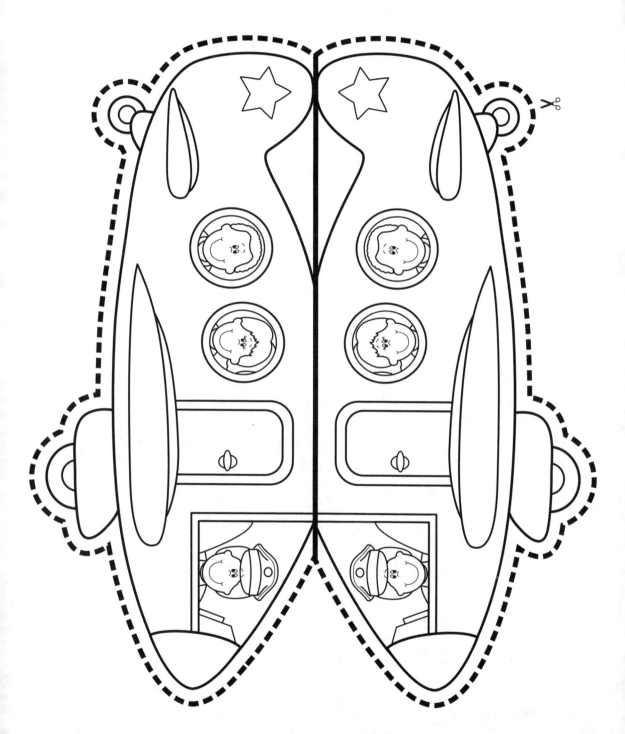

Cut on the dashed lines to make a sun. Color the picture.

Cut out the puzzle pieces on the dashed lines. Arrange the pieces correctly and paste them on a sheet of paper. Color the picture.

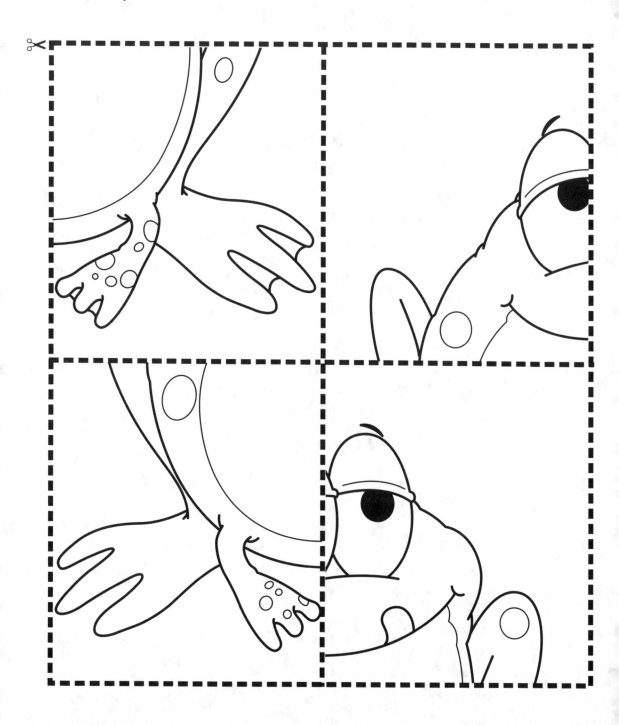

Color the bus. Then, cut on the dashed line and fold on the thick line. The bus will stand up.

Cut out the flowers on the dashed lines. Paste them on the picture. Color the picture.

© Carson-Dellosa CD-4511

Cut out the puzzle pieces on the dashed lines. Arrange the pieces correctly and paste them on a sheet of paper. Color the picture.

31

Cut out the rectangle. Fold it on the thick line. Then, cut on the dashed line. What shape is this?

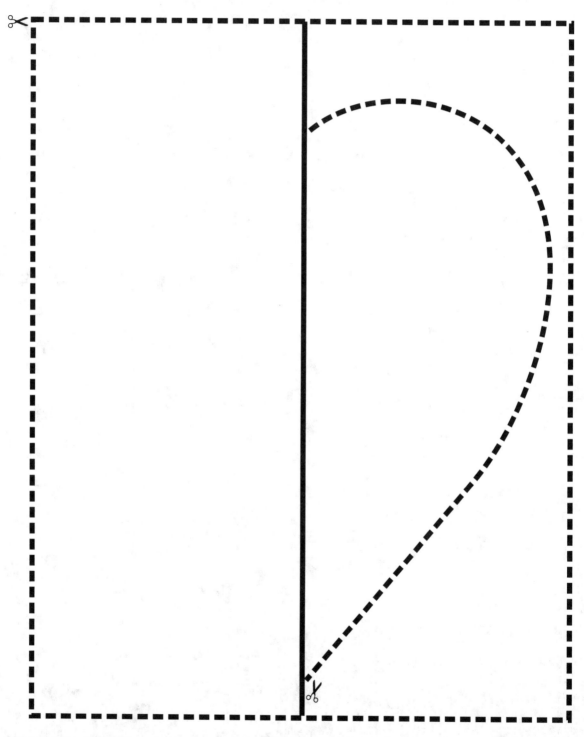

Cut out the puzzle pieces on the dashed lines. Arrange the pieces correctly and paste them on a sheet of paper. Color the picture.

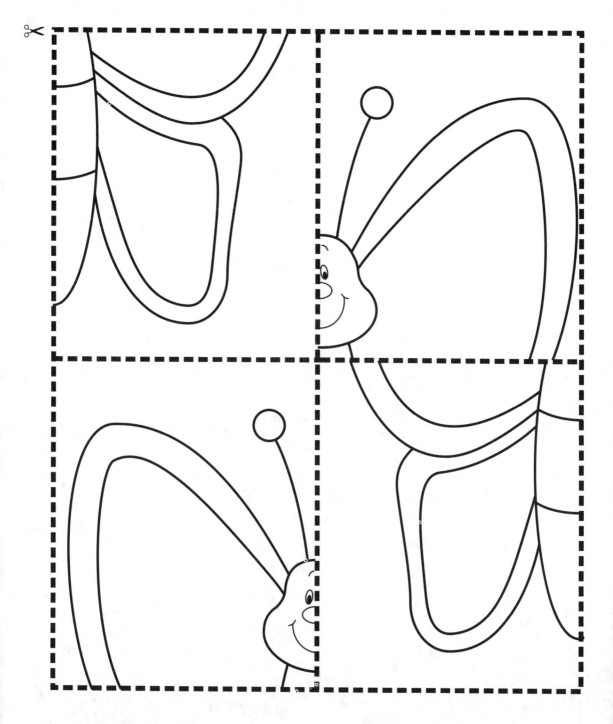

Cut the dashed lines below.

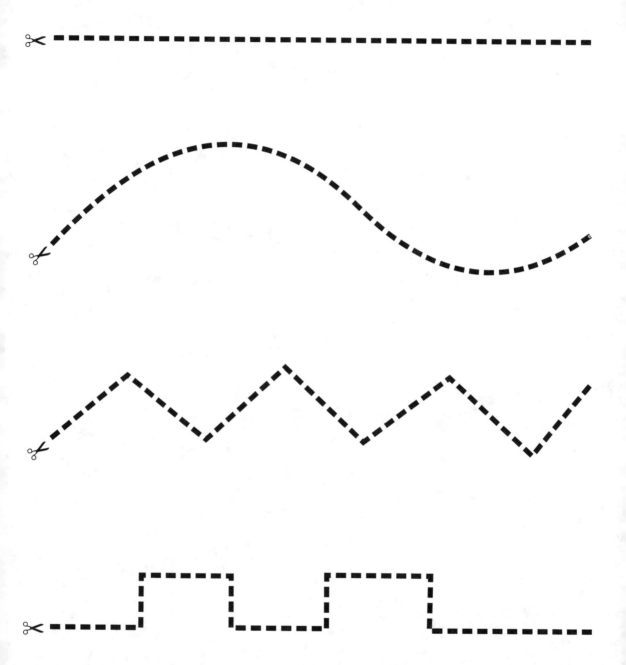

Cut the dashed lines below.

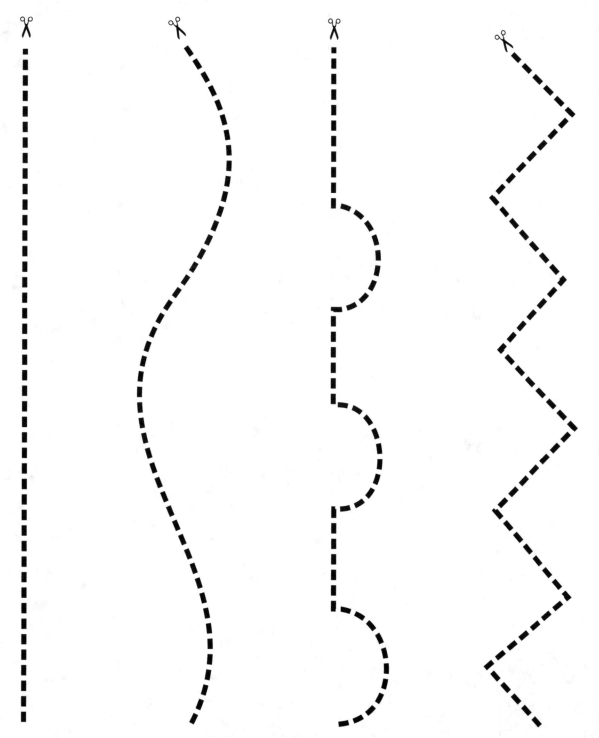

Cut out the pieces of the house on the dashed lines.
Paste them on the picture. Color the picture.

Cut out the balls on the dashed lines and paste them on the picture. Color the picture.

Cut out the ice cream scoops on the dashed lines and paste them on the picture. Color the picture.

45

Cut out the fish on the dashed lines and paste them in the bowl. Color the picture.

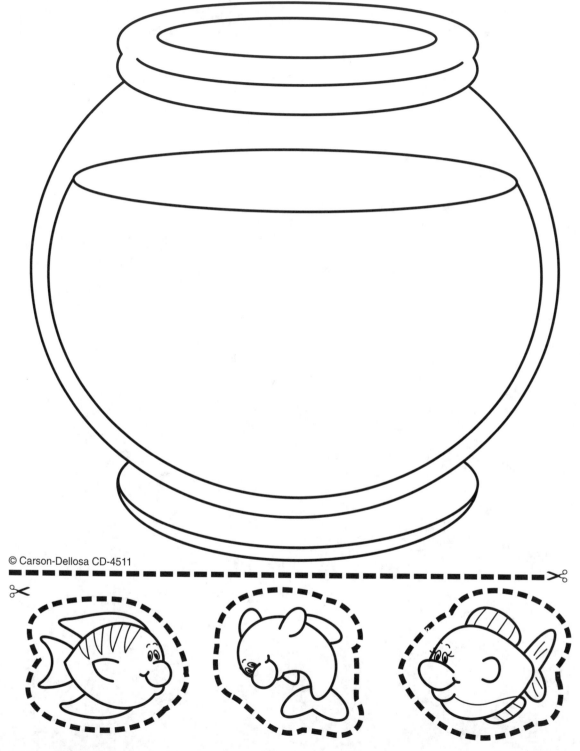

© Carson-Dellosa CD-4511

© Carson-Dellosa CD-4511

Cut out the apples on the dashed lines and paste them in the basket. Color the picture.

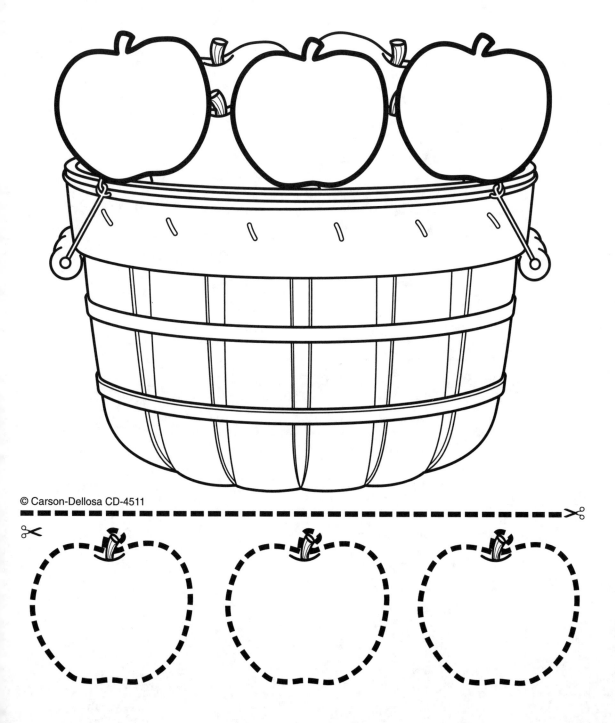

46

Cut out Nancy's hat on the dashed lines and paste it on her head. Color the picture.

Cut out Humpty Dumpty on the dashed lines and paste the pieces on the picture. Color the picture.

© Carson-Dellosa CD-4511

Cut out the parts of the clock on the dashed lines and paste them on the picture. Color the picture.

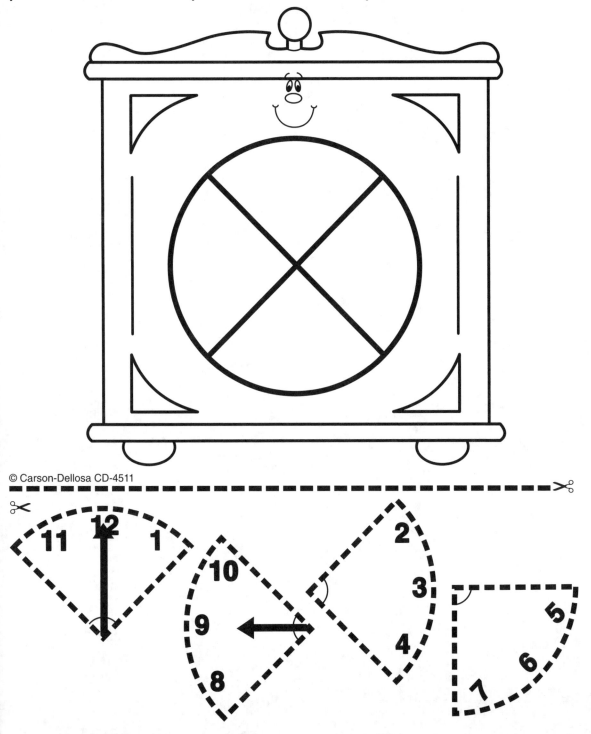

Cut out the pieces of the bear on the dashed lines.
Paste them into the scene on page 59.

Paste the bear from page 57 into the scene below.
Color the picture.

Cut out the pieces of the butterfly on the dashed lines.
Paste them into the scene on page 63.

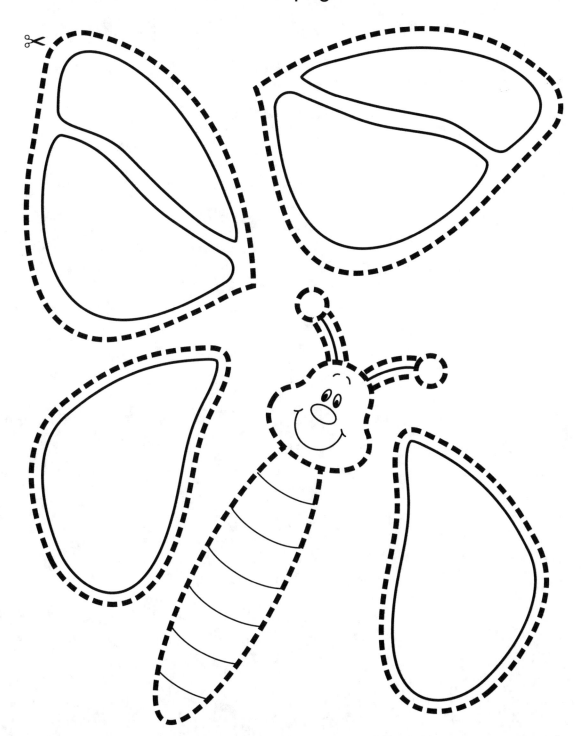

Paste the butterfly from page 61 into the scene below.
Color the picture.